Understanding Genetics™

The World of Microbes

Bacteria, Viruses, and Other Microorganisms

Janey Levy

ROSEN
PUBLISHING®

New York

Published in 2011 by The Rosen Publishing Group, Inc.
29 East 21st Street, New York, NY 10010

Copyright © 2011 by The Rosen Publishing Group, Inc.

First Edition

Library of Congress Cataloging-in-Publication Data

Levy, Janey.
The world of microbes: bacteria, viruses, and other microorganisms /
Janey Levy. — 1st ed.
        p. cm. — (Understanding genetics)
Includes bibliographical references and index.
ISBN 978-1-4358-9536-2 (library binding)
1. Bacteria—Juvenile literature. 2. Microorganisms—Juvenile literature. I. Title.
QR57.L48 2011
616.9'201—dc22

                                                                    2009048520

Manufactured in the United States of America

CPSIA Compliance Information: Batch #S10YA: For further information, contact Rosen Publishing, New York, New York, at 1-800-237-9932.

On the cover: This photograph of the microbe *Amoeba proteus*, magnified four hundred times, was taken with a scanning electron microscope. The organism is undergoing binary fission. The numerous fingerlike projections are its pseudopodia.

Contents

Introduction

Bacteria and viruses. For some people, those words produce fear. It's no wonder, given the news stories. Reporters recount alarming tales of flesh-eating bacteria and of people who died from food contaminated with the bacterium *Escherichia coli* (better known simply as *E. coli*). They announce fears of worldwide epidemics of viral diseases such as bird flu and swine flu. The stories can make it seem as if these microbes are out to get humans. Yet that's hardly true. In fact, as a group, they're more beneficial than harmful. Knowing more about them improves understanding of the good they do and the wealth of knowledge they offer—particularly about life processes and genetics.

Bacteria, archaea (once considered strange bacteria), and most protists (including the organisms commonly known as protozoans and some algae) are microbes. A microbe is a unicellular (single-celled) organism so small it can't be seen without a microscope. Viruses, which aren't cells, are even smaller—the term "microbe" applies to them, too. Microbes are everywhere. They're on Earth's surface, in the oceans, and underground. Famed naturalist E. O. Wilson gave a speech (which can be read in Tim Friend's book *The Third Domain*) in which he said the mass of microbes living underground may be greater than the combined mass of all living organisms on Earth's

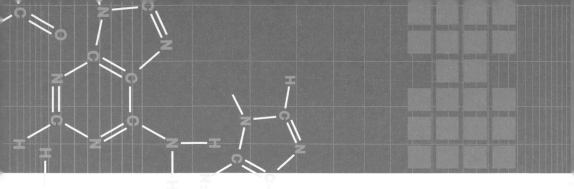

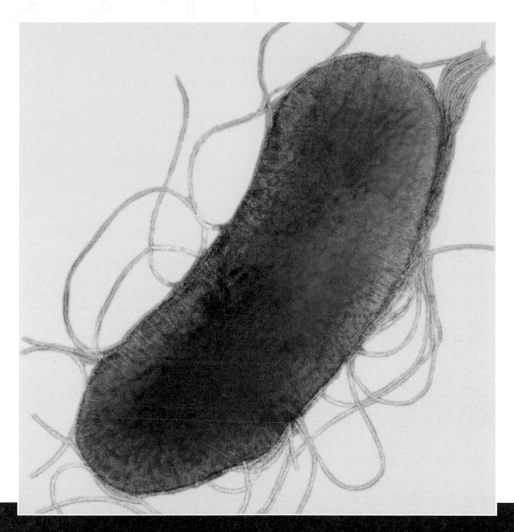

The bacterium Proteus mirabilis *is from 1 to 3 micrometers (.000039 to .000118 of an inch) long. Its numerous lengthy flagella are clearly visible. It's found in soil, water, and the human gut.*

surface. Microbes even live on and inside people. In fact, as micro-biologist Dorothy Crawford reports in *Deadly Companions*, one person may harbor 100,000,000,000,000 (that's 100 trillion) microbes. Crawford and Friend both note that this equals about ten microbes for each cell in the human body. Crawford calls microbes "deadly companions." While it's true that some microbes can sicken and kill people, it's hardly true that they all do. Many are helpful. Indeed, many are essential to human existence. Physician and writer Jeanette Farrell calls microbes "invisible allies" in her book of the same name.

Genetic studies of microbes have revealed much about life processes and the origin of life on Earth. Continued research will help scientists understand more about all life on Earth, including human life. How is it possible that the study of microbes could do all this? In part, it's because of a phenomenon called the conservation of genes across species. This simply means that the gene responsible for a specific task in one species will be very much like the gene responsible for that task in other species. So biologists can take what they learn about genes in microbes and apply it to other life-forms. Sure, scientists could use genes from any species. They don't have to use microbes. However, microbes can be grown quickly and cheaply in the laboratory, can be stored almost indefinitely, and are easy to work with. Before proceeding with the discussion of microbes, it's a good idea to begin with some basic concepts of genetics.

CHAPTER one

The Basics

Genetics is the branch of biology that studies heredity and variation in organisms. Like all fields of study, it has its own language. Anyone who wants to understand genetics must know at least a few key terms. An obvious place to start is the term "gene." Genes are commonly defined as the basic units of heredity. They're the cellular elements that determine what traits an organism, including a person, inherits from its parents.

Genes are located on cell structures called chromosomes. These are made of proteins and a substance called deoxyribonucleic acid, or DNA. An organism's complete set of DNA is its genome. However, a genome contains more than genes. Many DNA segments contain information unrelated to heredity. Individual genes are just DNA segments that tell the cell how to make the proteins necessary for life. For these instructions to be carried out, DNA needs help. This help comes from another substance called ribonucleic acid, or RNA. RNA takes DNA's instructions and helps the cell execute them. In some viruses, it replaces DNA as a carrier of genetic codes.

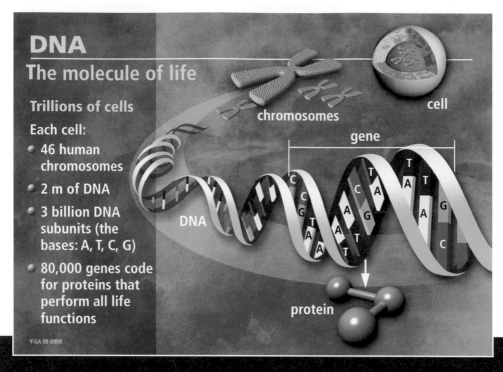

DNA
The molecule of life

Trillions of cells

Each cell:
- 46 human chromosomes
- 2 m of DNA
- 3 billion DNA subunits (the bases: A, T, C, G)
- 80,000 genes code for proteins that perform all life functions

Y-GA 98-090R

chromosomes

cell

gene

DNA

protein

This diagram clearly shows the spiral-ladder structure of DNA. It also shows the pairings of the bases that form the ladder's rungs: A and T, G and C.

A Brief History of Genetics

The history of genetics began with the work of Austrian botanist and monk Gregor Mendel in the 1850s. Mendel's experiments on the heredity of traits in pea plants led him to work out the basic rules governing how information is passed from one generation to the next. Mendel published his work in 1866, but it went largely unnoticed until 1900, when it was rediscovered by botanists Carl Erich Correns, Erich Tschermak von Seysenegg, and Hugo de Vries. That was shortly after the discovery of chromosomes. Microscopes made that discovery possible. The compound microscope was invented around 1590. However, it wasn't until the 1800s, when better glass-making methods yielded improved microscopes, that scientists could see inside cells and discover chromosomes.

Chromosomes and Heredity

Studies of cells and cell reproduction persuaded some scientists that chromosomes were the basis of heredity, although no experimental evidence existed. Proof came from experiments by biologist Thomas Hunt Morgan. Beginning in 1909, Morgan led a team of scientists investigating the inheritance of traits over several generations. The scientists used fruit flies because they grow and reproduce rapidly and possess numerous traits that can be easily tracked over

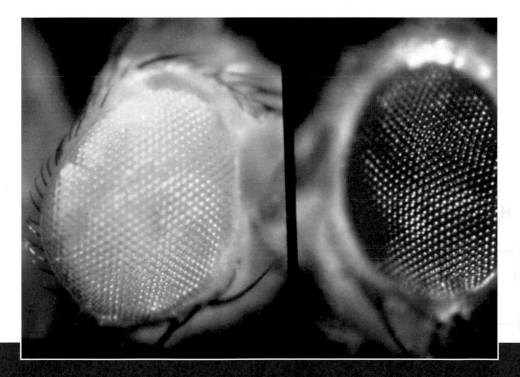

These greatly magnified images show a normal fruit fly eye on the right. Genetic mutations have resulted in a lack of pigment in the eye on the left.

generations. Their research demonstrated that genes are the units of heredity and are located on chromosomes.

Morgan and his team also produced the first genetic map. Mutations (genetic changes) are easily observed in fruit flies. The mutations helped the scientists determine each gene's location and the trait it affected.

In the 1940s, biologist George W. Beadle and biochemist Edward L. Tatum demonstrated how genes work. Their experiments on a mold (a kind of fungus) showed how genes direct the production of special proteins called enzymes, which control chemical reactions in cells. The men also established that each gene controls the production of one specific enzyme. Yet a question remained: Which material in chromosomes made up the genes?

DNA

Scientists had long known that chromosomes contain proteins and DNA. Yet DNA—discovered by biologist Johann Friedrich Miescher in 1869—was largely ignored. Life processes require proteins, and most scientists believed chromosomal proteins determined heredity. That view prevailed until 1944, when the bacterial DNA experiments of physician Oswald T. Avery and a team of scientists demonstrated that DNA decides heredity.

So what exactly is DNA? It's composed of chemical building blocks called nucleotides. Nucleotides contain three components: a phosphate group, a sugar (deoxyribose), and a base. Since all nucleotides are identical except for their bases, scientists identify them by their base. The four DNA bases are adenine (A), guanine (G), thymine (T), and cytosine (C).

In 1953, biologists James Watson and Francis Crick proposed that DNA is a double helix, which resembles a ladder twisted into a spiral. The phosphate and sugar molecules form the strong sides of the ladder. The rungs of the ladder are created by weak chemical bonds between the bases. Chemical rules govern how the bases bond. A always bonds with T; G always bonds with C.

The Genetic Code

By 1953, scientists knew genes were bits of DNA that carried a code telling the cell how to make proteins. However, they couldn't read the code.

By 1961, scientists had determined that the nucleotides in DNA were arranged in groups of three, which they called codons. Each codon instructs the cell to insert an amino acid, one of the building blocks of proteins. Scientists then set out to determine which codon corresponds to which amino acid.

In 1962, young biochemist Marshall W. Nirenberg identified the codon for one amino acid. Soon, scientists had identified the codons for all twenty amino acids in the proteins of living organisms. This meant they could begin to understand each gene's function and eventually recognize a mutation by its nucleotide sequence.

Most mutations make it less likely an organism will survive or reproduce. Rarely, however, they improve an organism's chance of survival and reproduction. In a species such as humans, most mutations affect only the individual in which they occur. Mutations are passed on to the next generation only if they occur in the cells that produce eggs or sperm. Because of the way archaea, bacteria, and viruses reproduce, however, any mutation can be passed on. So how do they reproduce, anyway?

Reproduction in Microbes

Two basic types of reproduction exist—sexual and asexual. Many microbes, including archaea and bacteria, generally reproduce asexually. Others reproduce sexually, and some can reproduce both ways. Viruses are a special case, since they reproduce only inside living cells.

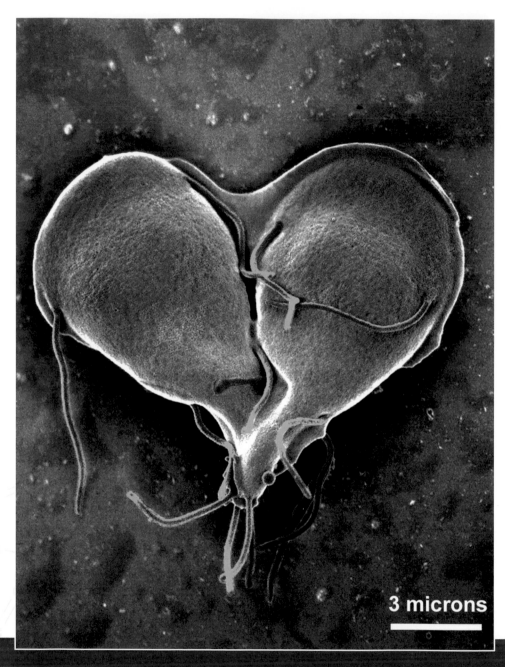

3 microns

Here, a Giardia lamblia protozoan undergoes binary fission. This protozoan causes a diarrheal disease called giardiasis. The image, taken with a scanning electron microscope, has been colored digitally.

Asexual reproduction involves a single parent. Microbes mostly reproduce through binary fission. The microbe copies its genome, then splits into two identical cells. Yeasts and some other microbes reproduce through budding. A cell produces a small, attached growth, or bud. The "daughter" cell is a genetic duplicate of the "mother" cell and eventually breaks off. Some microbes can also reproduce through fragmentation. The parent cell breaks into pieces, or fragments. Each fragment grows into a complete new microbe.

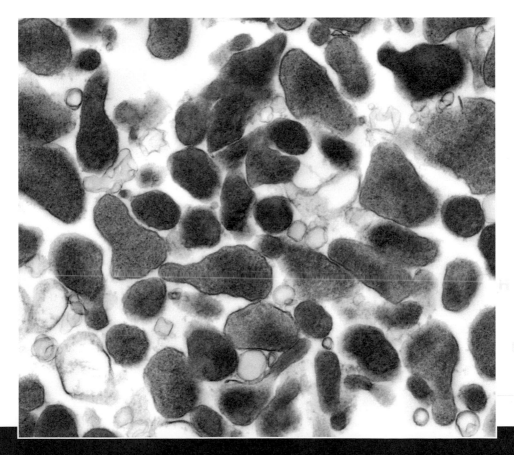

Mycoplasma genitalium *was the second bacterium to have its genome mapped. Its genome is the smallest among all living organisms. This image magnifies the bacterium more than forty thousand times.*

The Brave New World of Genetics

The study of genetics has advanced by leaps and bounds since the 1970s. First, scientists developed recombinant DNA technology—the removal of genes from one organism and insertion of them into another. Experiments using the technology have enabled scientists to learn more about genes' structure and function.

Another big development was genome sequencing—the process of determining the sequence, or order, of the nucleotides in an organism's DNA and identifying the genes. In 1977, two viruses were sequenced. In 1984, scientists sequenced the first virus that causes illness in humans, the Epstein-Barr virus. *Haemophilus influenzae* became the first bacterium sequenced in 1995. The following year, the first

Watson and Crick

James Watson was born in Chicago, Illinois, in 1928. He studied at the University of Chicago and Indiana University. In 1951, he began working at Cambridge University's Cavendish Laboratory in England, where he met Francis Crick.

Crick was born in Northampton, England, in 1916. He studied at University College, London, and Cambridge University and joined the Cavendish Laboratory in 1949. After Watson's arrival, the two began working together to determine DNA's structure. Their double-helix model earned them (and biophysicist Maurice Wilkins of King's College, London) the 1962 Nobel Prize in Physiology or Medicine. Crick later spearheaded the field of molecular biology. He died in 2004. Watson was a leader in the Human Genome Project (the international effort to sequence the human genome), which he headed at the National Institutes of Health until 1992.

archaean (*Methanococcus jannaschii*) was sequenced. The first protist—*Cyanidioschyzon merolae*, a unicellular red alga—was sequenced in 2004.

Why does genome sequencing matter? It helps scientists understand individual species, clarifies relationships between species, and provides insight into evolutionary history. It improves understanding of how organisms work. It can help scientists and doctors better understand the genetic causes of diseases, resulting in better diagnosis and treatment methods.

That's all well and good, the reader might think, but does it really matter if microbial genomes are sequenced? It does. Understanding the genomes of disease-causing microbes may inspire new treatments. Knowing the genomes of beneficial microbes may yield improved ways to use them. Finally, remember the concept of conservation of genes across species discussed in the introduction? Whether people like it or not, humans and microbes share DNA. What scientists learn from microbes can increase knowledge of humans.

CHAPTER two

Meet the Microbes

The traditional scientific classification system for organisms—no longer used by evolutionary biologists—has eight main levels, or taxa. Each level is smaller (lower) than the one before (above) it. The highest taxon is the domain. Three domains exist—Bacteria, Archaea, and Eukarya (sometimes called Eukaryota). The first two are entirely microbes, and the third includes some microbes. What determines which domain an organism belongs in? Cell features are important factors.

Two basic cell types exist—eukaryotic and prokaryotic. Plants and animals (including humans) have eukaryotic cells. A thin membrane surrounds their cytoplasm, which contains the nucleus and small structures called organelles. The nucleus is the cell's control center and holds the chromosomes. A membrane encloses it. The organelles perform various important functions.

Prokaryotic cells are much smaller than eukaryotic cells. Most have a cell wall around the cell membrane. They contain cytoplasm but have no nucleus. Instead, they have a nucleoid, which lacks a surrounding membrane.

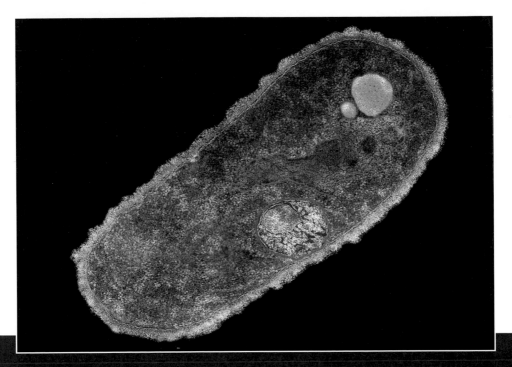

This electron microscope image of the bacterium Bacillus megaterium *clearly shows the various prokaryotic cell parts: cell wall (orange), cell membrane (blue), nucleoid (pink), and organelles (turquoise and red-orange).*

Bacteria and archaea are prokaryotic unicellular organisms. The domain Eukarya contains eukaryotic unicellular protists as well as multicellular protists, fungi, plants, and animals.

The observant reader will have noticed that viruses haven't been mentioned. These tiny, simple organisms are major causes of disease. Where do they fit in the classification system? Keep reading to learn more.

Bacteria

Bacteria (once called "eubacteria," meaning "true bacteria") may be spherical, rod shaped, or spiral. They may have flagella. They may

Some bacteria survive in unfavorable conditions by forming spores and becoming inactive until conditions become favorable again. This image shows spores and vegetative, or growing, cells of Bacillus anthracis (which causes anthrax disease).

be linked together. Bacteria live everywhere—on and in soil, in the oceans, inside plants and animals.

Bacteria are among Earth's oldest life-forms. Billions of years ago, Earth had a very different environment. Bacteria that could thrive in extreme environments populated the planet. Extreme environments include those that are much hotter, colder, or saltier than most modern life-forms could endure.

Extreme forms of bacteria still exist, which means bacteria can be found even where scientists once thought nothing could survive. They live in steaming hot springs, ice, and solid rocks. They live on and in people. Compared to such astounding adaptability, humans are frail beings.

Unicellular Fungi

The domain Eukarya includes fungi as well as protists. The word "fungi" usually makes people picture readily visible organisms such as mushrooms. Yet most fungi are microscopic.

People are usually familiar with microscopic fungi even if they don't realize it. Yeasts, for example, belong to this group. Some cause illnesses in animals and plants, but others are beneficial. Many people, in fact, consume yeast daily. It's an essential ingredient in making bread and beer.

Most people have seen mold growing on fruit or bread, so it may be a surprise to learn that molds can also be microscopic. What people see on fruit or bread is a colony, not an individual mold. Like yeasts, molds can cause disease or be beneficial. Some are used in making cheese. Others yield medicines such as penicillin.

People commonly consider bacteria as enemies to be destroyed. It's true some cause terrible, even fatal, diseases. Yet most are either harmless or beneficial. Bacteria have helped create an environment on Earth that makes human life possible. Many bacteria live inside humans without causing harm. Others perform vital functions without which people wouldn't survive. In fact, without those bacteria that generated oxygen gas by photosynthesis, there would never have been people. Chapter 4 provides a more in-depth look at bacteria. Now it's time to meet another ancient microbe.

Archaea

Archaea weren't even recognized as distinct from bacteria until the late 1970s. When first discovered, they were widely

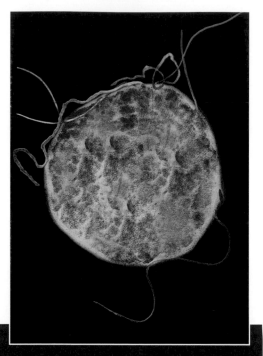

The archaeon Sulfolobus acidocaldarius is an extremophile found in hot springs in Yellowstone National Park. It prefers highly acidic environments with temperatures of around 176 degrees Fahrenheit (80 degrees Celsius).

considered strange bacteria and called archaebacteria. However, genetic studies later revealed that their ancestors diverged from bacteria nearly four billion years ago. Since the existing classification system had no place for them, scientists created the domain Archaea.

Archaea may be spherical, rod shaped, or even square or triangular. They may have flagella.

Archaea live everywhere. The extremophiles—lovers of extremes—are perhaps the most famous. Like bacteria, they inhabit solid ice and steaming, sometimes highly acidic, hot springs. They live deep inside Earth's rocky surface, beneath the hottest desert sands, and in the thin, cold atmosphere high above Earth. They dwell in oil wells and methane pools. They live in animals' (including humans') digestive systems.

For Earth's first three billion years, archaea dominated the planet. These were extremophiles that could thrive in the extreme conditions existing then. Archaea are still extremely common. They may, in fact, be the most common microbes in the soil today. Chapter 5 examines archaea more closely. Now it's time to meet the protists.

The Tree of Life

This diagram shows a very simple version of the tree of life, which shows how different groups of organisms are related and when groups separated. Many branches and twigs (especially of protists) are not shown, and the "complete" tree will surely be updated. New discoveries and new ways of thinking will force changes to the tree and generate disagreements among biologists.

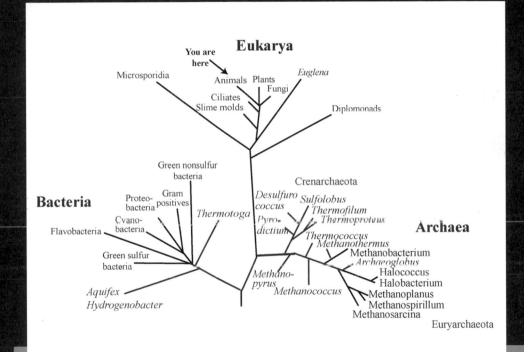

Charles Darwin produced an early tree of life diagram in the mid-1800s. Modern diagrams often don't look like trees, but they're still meant to show relationships among groups of organisms.

Protists

Protists belong to the domain Eukarya and possess typical eukaryotic cells. Most protists are microscopic, unicellular organisms. Like other microbes, they live almost everywhere. Some live independently, some have a symbiotic lifestyle, and others are disease-causing parasites. Familiar protists include algae and protozoans.

Protists are an odd group. In the late 1900s, biologists assigned numerous eukaryotes to the kingdom Protista, whose name means "the very first." They believed these organisms were primitive beings that first appeared about two billion years ago. However, genome analysis has shown that the ancestors of some protists were more complex than the modern organisms. It has also revealed that many protists aren't closely related to each other and thus don't really belong together in a single kingdom. But they don't belong with any other eukaryotes either. They're not animals, plants, or fungi. So, for the sake of convenience, scientists continue to use the terms "Protista" and "protist." Chapter 6 offers a closer look at protists. Now it's time to meet that most curious of microbes, the virus.

Viruses

Viruses are strange microbes. Like other microbes, they're found everywhere and come in many shapes. Unlike other microbes, however, almost all viruses cause diseases in humans, other animals, plants, and even bacteria. Their definition also distinguishes them from other microbes. A virus is defined as a microscopic organism that lives inside a cell of another organism, called the host. The key words here are "lives inside." That's because a virus can only reproduce—an essential property of living things—when it's inside another organism's cell.

Why does a virus have to be inside a host's cell to reproduce? It's because of its structure. A virus isn't composed of cells or even a single

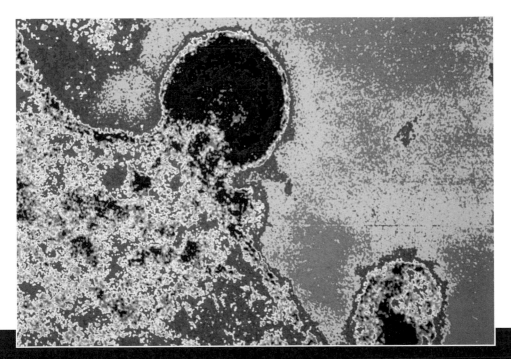

The dark circle at the top is the human immunodeficiency virus (HIV), which causes acquired immunodeficiency syndrome (AIDS). It's fusing with an immune system cell and injecting its RNA into the cell.

cell. It consists solely of a nucleic acid core and a protein sheath, or coating. Without cytoplasm and its contents, it lacks the tools to reproduce. So it takes over the machinery of another organism's cell to carry out this function. A few viruses seem to do this without harming their host. Usually, however, viruses make the host ill, sometimes fatally.

Because of viruses' primitive structure, scientists can't agree whether they're living or not. Many consider viruses to have *both* living and nonliving characteristics.

CHAPTER three

A Brief History of Microbiology

Microbiology is the study of microbes, also called microscopic organisms or microorganisms. Because microbiology requires microscopes, its history encompasses that of microscopes. That history began with the earliest lenses.

According to the Paper Project, ancient Egyptians made lenses from rock crystal about 4,600 years ago. Microscope.com reports that the Chinese used lenses consisting of water in a tube about 4,000 years ago.

Wearable eyeglasses were invented late in the 1200s. Then, around 1590, Dutch eyeglass maker Zacharias Janssen invented the compound microscope, which combined the power of two or more sets of lenses. Scientists discovered a whole new world.

A Miniature World Revealed

Two important names in early microbiology are Robert Hooke and Antoni van Leeuwenhoek. Both men worked in the second half of the 1600s. Hooke gave us the word "cell." Leeuwenhoek was one of the first to see microbes. Their discoveries transformed scientists' understanding of the world.

Robert Hooke

English experimental scientist Robert Hooke (1635–1703) devised an illuminated compound microscope that was one of the best microscopes of the time. Although Hooke often left experiments unfinished, he contributed to numerous scientific fields. In biology, his reputation rests largely on his 1665 book entitled *Micrographia*. *Micrographia* contains written descriptions of what Hooke observed through his microscope. He coined the word "cell" to describe what he saw

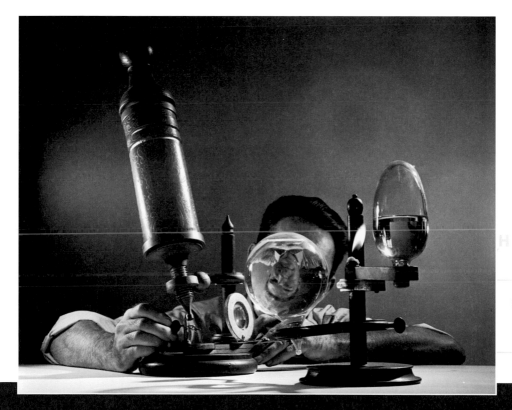

This model of Robert Hooke's illuminated compound microscope was based on plans in his book Micrographia. *The model was built around 1950 at the Cleveland Health Museum.*

when he examined a thin slice of cork. The book also contains highly detailed engravings based on Hooke's drawings of the world his microscope revealed.

Antoni van Leeuwenhoek

The remarkable Antoni van Leeuwenhoek (1632–1723) wasn't a scientist but a Dutch cloth merchant. Oddly enough, his extraordinary scientific discoveries resulted from his humble profession.

Leeuwenhoek needed lenses to inspect cloth. He became a highly skilled lens maker and created simple microscopes with his lenses. Although difficult to use, their magnification was about ten times greater than contemporary compound microscopes. With them, Leeuwenhoek discovered tiny organisms he called "animalcules" ("tiny animals"). He was the first to see protozoans and to clearly describe bacteria and red blood cells. Leeuwenhoek's descriptions are so accurate that most are instantly recognizable to scientists today.

The Fight Against Microbes and Disease

In the 1600s, people believed illnesses resulted from miasmas—bad air from swamps, dead bodies, and such. Leeuwenhoek suggested his animalcules were the cause. This idea, called the germ theory, wasn't new. More than a century earlier—before microbes were discovered—Italian doctor Girolamo Fracastoro had suggested that tiny "seeds" spread infectious diseases. However, Fracastoro lacked proof. Even Leeuwenhoek's discovery wasn't enough. Belief in miasmas lasted until the mid-1800s.

Edward Jenner

English doctor Edward Jenner (1749–1823) regularly confronted smallpox. This viral disease covers the body with painful, pus-filled bumps called pustules (pox). Today the virus exists only in research laboratories. Over the centuries, however, it killed hundreds of

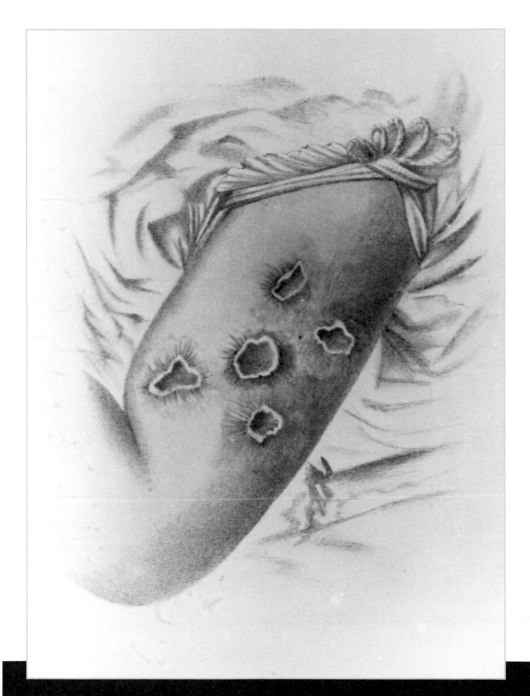

This 1898 illustration shows a reaction to the smallpox vaccine on a young person's upper arm. Such reactions were expected to occur eight days after vaccination.

millions of people and permanently harmed millions more. Although viruses were still unknown, Jenner found a safe, effective way to prevent smallpox.

Dairymaids who caught the minor disease cowpox seemed immune to smallpox. In 1796, Jenner took matter from a dairymaid's cowpox pustule and inserted it into cuts on a healthy boy's arm. The boy caught cowpox but recovered. Jenner later inserted smallpox matter into the boy's arm. The boy remained healthy. Cowpox had made him immune to smallpox. Jenner called the treatment "vaccination," from the Latin word for cow, *vacca*.

Louis Pasteur

French chemist Louis Pasteur (1822–1895) earned his fame from his work with microbes.

In 1857, Pasteur proved microbes cause fermentation—an essential process in producing wine, beer, yogurt, and cheese. He discovered that some microbes function only when oxygen isn't present. He called them "anaerobic." He called organisms that require oxygen "aerobic." In 1859,

The Theory of Spontaneous Generation

Since ancient times, people had believed in spontaneous generation—the idea that some life-forms sprang from nonliving matter. Leeuwenhoek hoped his discovery of animalcules would disprove spontaneous generation. Yet people couldn't let go of the long-held theory. Belief in spontaneous generation lasted until the mid-1800s.

he disproved spontaneous generation. In 1863, he developed pasteurization—the use of heat to kill food-spoiling microbes.

In 1879, Pasteur demonstrated that the bacterium *Bacillus anthracis* causes anthrax, proving the germ theory. Two years later, he had an effective anthrax vaccine. He began studying rabies in 1882. Because a virus causes rabies, Pasteur couldn't see it. Nevertheless, he had an experimental vaccine in 1885 when desperate parents begged him to try it on their young son. A rabid dog had bitten the boy. Pasteur agreed to vaccinate the boy, and he saved the child's life.

Robert Koch

German physician Robert Koch (1843–1910) is less famous than Pasteur but equally important. Although neither man knew it, Koch

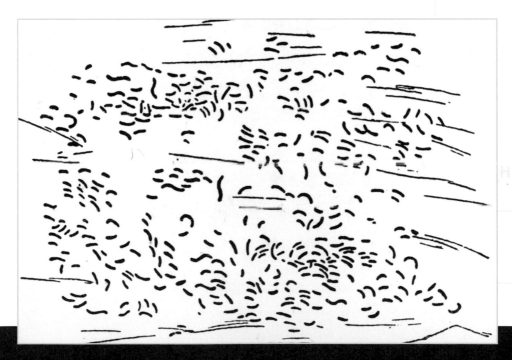

Robert Koch drew this sketch of Vibrio cholerae, *which was exhibited at a conference held in 1884, the year after he identified the bacterium as the cause of cholera.*

was studying anthrax at the same time Pasteur was. Like Pasteur, Koch demonstrated that *Bacillus anthracis* causes anthrax.

In 1877, Koch published his method for preparing bacteria for study under a microscope. He also outlined Koch's postulates—a series of steps for determining if a particular microbe causes a particular disease. These steps are still used today.

In 1882, Koch discovered that the bacterium *Mycobacterium tuberculosis* causes the often-fatal disease tuberculosis. In 1883, he identified the bacterium *Vibrio cholerae* as the cause of cholera. He received the 1905 Nobel Prize in Physiology or Medicine for his work on tuberculosis.

The Search for Hidden Disease Agents

Despite the progress, scientists couldn't find causes for illnesses such as measles, yellow fever, smallpox, and rabies (remember, Jenner and Pasteur didn't know what caused smallpox and rabies). Other diseases with unknown causes destroyed livestock and crops.

Discoveries around 1900 yielded new hope. In 1898, Dutch microbiologist Martinus Beijerinck

Joseph Lister

Surgery was quite risky before the 1860s. Infections often followed even minor operations. Almost half of all surgery patients died.

English doctor Joseph Lister (1827–1912) changed that. After Pasteur's discoveries, Lister realized microbes caused infections following surgery. He insisted that antiseptics—germ-killing agents—be used on hands, instruments, and dressings (bandages). These practices immediately reduced the number of infections in surgical patients.

was researching a tobacco plant disease. He strained juice from diseased leaves through a filter whose tiny pores prevented the passage of all known bacteria. Yet the filtered juice still spread the disease. Beijerinck called the disease-causing agent a liquid, living virus, from the Latin word for poison. Russian biologist Dmitri Ivanovski was also studying the disease. He concluded the agent was an extremely tiny particle, not a liquid.

Whatever it was, no microscope of the time was powerful enough to reveal it. That would eventually change.

A New Age in Microbiology

Since the early 1900s, advances in microbiology have transformed the way scientists think about the origin and development of life. Progress in the study of genetics, discussed in chapter 1, played an important role. So did developments in microscopes.

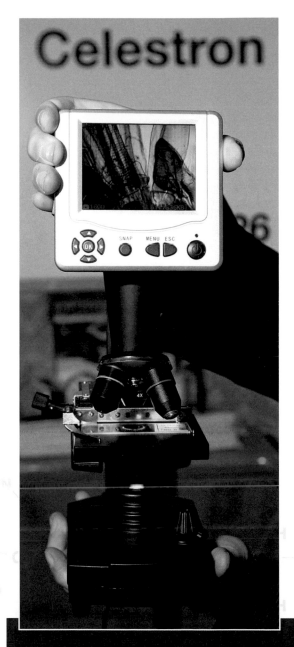

This digital microscope was presented at an electronics show in 2008. It has up to 1600 zoom and can send images to a computer screen.

This 1961 photograph shows a young Carl Woese more than a decade before the microbiologist identified the domain Archaea. He's holding a model of RNA.

Advances in Microscopes

The electron microscope was invented in 1931. By shooting electrons at the object being studied, it can magnify objects up to one million times! However, because objects must be put into a vacuum, living cells can't be examined.

The ion microscope, invented in 1951, allowed scientists to look at individual atoms. In the early 1980s, two new microscopes appeared. The environmental scanning electron microscope may some day allow scientists to study living cells. The scanning tunneling microscope permitted researchers to obtain three-dimensional images of metal surfaces at an atomic level. More recently, digital microscopes send images directly to computer screens.

Amazing Microbes

During this same period, other scientists developed new ideas and discovered new categories of microbes. When Russia launched the first *Sputnik* satellite in 1957, most scientists thought life in the extreme environment of space was impossible. Microbiologist Joshua Lederberg disagreed and wondered what would happen if a spacecraft brought alien microbes back to Earth. Then, in 1992, physicist Thomas Gold argued that billions of microbes populate Earth's interior. Most scientists at the time judged this ridiculous. It's now considered fact. What changed? Extremophiles were discovered.

In the 1960s, scientists began finding microbes in extreme environments—hot springs, deep-ocean vents where water temperature and pressure are extremely high, and extremely cold places. Then, in the 1970s, something else astounding happened. Microbiologist Carl Woese determined that many of these extremophiles belonged to an entirely new domain—Archaea. Once again, a new world opened up.

CHAPTER four

A World Brimming with Bacteria

Bacteria are one of Earth's oldest life-forms. How do scientists know? Fossils provide some evidence. Yes, even microbes can leave fossils. Earth's oldest known fossils are 3.5-billion-year-old prokaryotes.

Bacteria range in size from about 0.2 to 10 micrometers, according to physician and researcher Frank Lowy. How small is that? One inch equals more than twenty-five thousand micrometers!

Bacteria may be spherical, rod shaped, or spiral. Thousands of species are known, and millions may exist.

Bacteria live even where life seems impossible. Extremophiles live in ice and around deep-sea vents, where temperatures surpass the boiling point and the pressure is crushing. Billions of bacteria dwell deep inside Earth, without air and sunlight. These are the SLIMES. "SLIMES" stands for subterranean lithoautotrophic microbial ecosystems. "Subterranean" simply means below Earth's surface. "Lithoautotrophic" means getting its energy from minerals rather than organic material.

Antarctica, the coldest, iciest place on Earth, seems totally inhospitable to life. Yet extremophiles have been found there.

So, how many bacteria exist on Earth? In *Deadly Companions*, Crawford writes that a single ounce (30 milliliters) of seawater contains at least thirty million!

Good Bacteria

Many advertisements urge people to protect their families by using antibacterial products. The message is clear: Bacteria are bad. Yet most bacteria are harmless or even beneficial to humans. In fact, ancient bacteria helped make all eukaryotic life possible. When the first bacteria appeared billions of years ago, Earth was much hotter and its atmosphere lacked oxygen. Early bacteria called

Without a microscope, it's not possible to directly observe bacterial decomposers at work. These mushrooms (a type of fungi) growing on a tree stump provide an opportunity to watch decomposers in action.

cyanobacteria changed conditions by performing photosynthesis, releasing oxygen as a waste product. Modern bacteria still do many useful things.

Decomposers and Recyclers

Every organism dies. If the life cycle stopped there, dead organisms would cover the planet, trapping essential nutrients. New life couldn't begin. Decomposers, notably bacteria and fungi, break down dead organisms, releasing the nutrients to be recycled, or reused. One critical nutrient is nitrogen.

All organisms need nitrogen for their DNA and amino acids. Earth's atmosphere has plenty, but plants and animals can't use gaseous nitrogen. Bacteria help by performing a process called nitrogen fixation. Decomposers release ammonia. Other bacteria change ammonia into nitrogen compounds called nitrites, which others change into nitrates. Plants get nitrogen from nitrates, and animals get it from plants.

Bacteria Make It Delicious

People may be unaware that they eat bacteria daily. Bacteria help make some of the human diet's most basic foods. For example, bread requires bacteria as well as yeast. Dairy foods such as cheese, butter, and yogurt need bacteria, too.

Bacteria are also used to make sausage and soy sauce. Perhaps most surprising is that bacteria help create many people's favorite sweet—chocolate!

Other Benefits from Bacteria

Bacteria provide other benefits. Some feast on human and animal waste. They're used to clean wastewater. Still others eat oil and are used to clean up oil spills. Bacteria help control insect pests, too.

Drug companies use bacteria to make medicines and vitamins. They even make antibiotics from bacteria!

Many researchers are investigating other beneficial uses for bacteria. These include fighting health problems such as intestinal disorders and cancer and producing fuel. Perhaps someday bacteria will power cars!

Bad Bacteria

"Bad" bacteria cause infections and diseases ranging from mild to fatal. They infect cuts and cause sore throats, ear infections, food poisoning, pneumonia, tuberculosis, and even stomach ulcers!

How can people fight harmful bacteria? Heat can kill them. Disinfectants can destroy bacteria in water and on surfaces and objects. Antiseptics can prevent infection in cuts and wounds. Doctors may give vaccines to prevent bacterial diseases or prescribe antibiotics to treat them. Unfortunately, overuse of antibiotics has created drug-resistant bacteria. This means infections and diseases that were once easy to treat can now become quite serious. Scientists are seeking new ways to fight these bacteria.

Symbiotic Bacteria

Some bacteria have symbiotic relationships with plants or animals. In symbiosis, two organisms live in a close, mutually beneficial union.

Remember bacteria's role in nitrogen recycling? This talent produced a symbiotic relationship between bacteria and plants. Bacteria called rhizobia infect the roots of certain plants. They supply nitrogen for the plants and get their needs met in return.

Many animals have symbiotic relationships with bacteria. For example, tiny insects called aphids eat sap, which lacks amino acids. Bacteria inside their cells produce amino acids for the aphids and get energy and nutrients in return. The Hawaiian squid provides a home for special light-producing bacteria. The squid uses the light to camouflage itself.

People have symbiotic relationships with bacteria, too. Bacteria inside the human mouth get nutrients and protect people from disease-causing microbes. Bacteria in human intestines help with digestion and receive essential nutrients.

Symbiosis contributed to the development of plants and animals. Chloroplasts in plant and some protist cells and mitochondria in all eukaryotic cells produce energy. Chloroplasts are the descendants of an ancient cyanobacterium. Mitochondria are what's left of an ancient proteobacterium.

Classifying Bacteria

How are bacteria classified? One method uses shape—cocci (spherical), bacilli (rod shaped), and spirilla (spiral). Another relies on whether they're aerobic or anaerobic.

Another method depends on their reaction to the Gram stain (a purple dye). The bacteria are stained with the dye, then washed with chemicals. Thin-walled bacteria remain purple and are called gram positive. Thick-walled bacteria lose the dye and are called gram negative.

But shape, metabolism, and Gram staining tell us nothing about relationships among different bacteria. The key to classification lies in sequencing RNA or DNA.

Cells contain ribosomes, where proteins are manufactured. Carl Woese used the 16s ribosomal RNA (16s rRNA) gene to classify bacteria. Why? Because every prokaryote has this gene, and it doesn't vary much among species.

Many bacterial types exist. The largest group, Firmicutes, has almost 2,500 species. All are gram positive. Parasitic *Mycoplasma* are the tiniest bacteria. Actinobacteria are decomposers. Many yield valuable antibiotics. Proteobacteria are gram negative. The large group includes *E. coli*, many disease-causing bacteria, rhizobia, and bacteria perhaps closely related to mitochondria's ancestors.

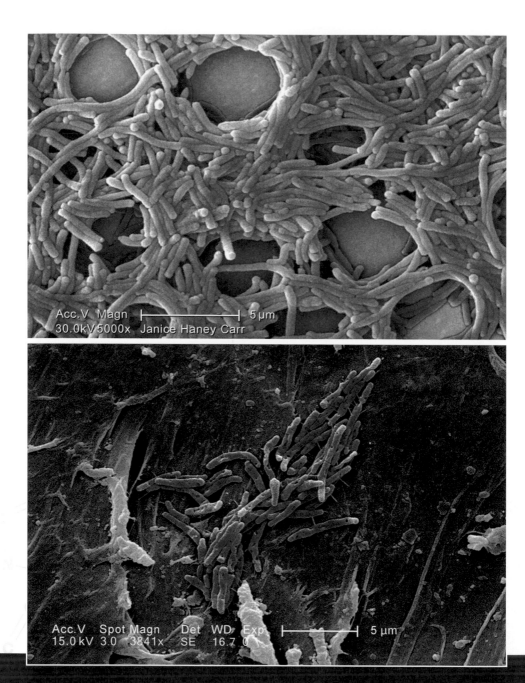

The top image shows gram-negative, rod-shaped Legionella pneumophila *bacteria. The purple forms in the center of the bottom image are gram-positive, rod-shaped* Mycobacterium fortuitum *bacteria.*

Bacteroidetes include the gram-negative, anaerobic bacteria that inhabit the human intestine. Cyanobacteria carry out photosynthesis. One ancient cyanobacterium was the ancestor of all chloroplasts.

Structure of Bacteria

Just as skin covers humans, cell walls enclose most bacteria. The rigid walls contain a material called peptidoglycan, which is stained by the Gram stain. Just inside is a membrane. Gram-negative bacteria have a membrane outside the wall, too—and usually less peptidoglycan in the wall. A slimy capsule surrounds everything.

Cytoplasm fills the interior. It contains enzymes that help in digestion and building parts, storage bodies called inclusions, nutrients, RNA, and DNA. A bacterium's nucleoid holds a single, circular chromosome. The cytoplasm may also contain smaller DNA bits called plasmids. Plasmids often carry genes for fighting antibiotics.

Many bacteria have one or more flagella attached to the outside to help them move. Some bacteria also have hair-like structures called pili that help them attach to each other and to the host.

Special Skills

Recent research has revealed some amazing bacterial abilities. Despite their rigid walls, bacteria are quite elastic. They can flatten themselves to pass through extremely tiny openings, then regain their normal shape. Bacteria can also communicate! They release chemicals into their surroundings to learn about their environment and communicate the information to other bacteria in the colony. This helps the colony—such as plaque that can form on your teeth— adapt and survive.

Because bacteria reproduce asexually, they don't have special reproductive structures. (Most bacteria reproduce through binary fission, although cyanobacteria can use budding and fragmentation.) However, some bacteria use pili to connect and exchange bits of DNA in a process called conjugation.

Bacterial Genomes

As chapter 1 mentioned, scientists first sequenced a bacterial genome in 1995. Now, sequencing bacteria seems so remote from everyday life that people may think, "So what? What difference does it make if scientists sequence bacterial genomes?" Well, it can make a big difference.

Knowing a bacterium's genome helps scientists understand the organism. That can help scientists discover more effective ways to fight bad bacteria and use beneficial bacteria. Since many bacteria have symbiotic relationships with plants and animals, knowing their genomes helps scientists understand the plants and animals and their needs better. Remember, too, that cellular organelles such as mitochondria and chloroplasts began as symbiotic bacteria. So everything scientists learn about bacteria helps them understand more about all life. Finally, think about this: it was sequencing ribosomes that led Carl Woese to the discovery of archaea, changed scientists' understanding of life, and opened a new universe of possibilities.

CHAPTER five

Ancient, Amazing Archaea

Like bacteria, archaea are ancient and left fossil evidence. Huge microbial mats of archaea and bacteria covered large sections of ocean floor with odd structures. What's a microbial mat? It's an immense collection of different microbe species. Microbes form mats because they're stronger and more efficient working together than as separate species.

Like bacteria, archaea are prokaryotic. Although they were originally considered weird bacteria, genetic studies revealed they're so different from bacteria that we now treat them as a separate domain. They were defined as a group in 1977, about three centuries after Leeuwenhoek observed bacteria.

It's impossible at this time to tell how many species of archaea (or, in fact, of bacteria) there are. Millions may exist. "Species" isn't easy to define for prokaryotes, which don't "breed" as do eukaryotes. In addition, bulk samples of seawater and soils contain DNA fragments that must come from staggering numbers of species. In any event, individual archaea are at least as numerous as

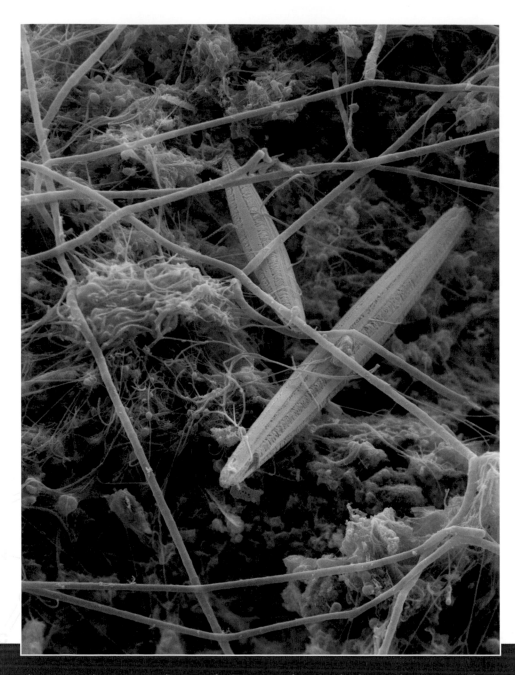

This image shows a greatly magnified portion of a microbial mat. The mats can form rocklike structures because microbes such as cyanobacteria secrete calcium carbonate, which hardens the mats.

bacteria. Tim Friend writes that a single drop of seawater holds a million or more!

Lifestyles of Archaea

Archaea live in the same places bacteria do—everywhere. They live on Earth's surface, in the soil and oceans, and deep underground in rock. Remember the SLIMES mentioned in chapter 4? Some archaea are SLIMES, just like some bacteria. Archaea live inside people. They can be aerobic or anaerobic. Many are extremophiles. These include thermophiles, or "lovers of heat." Some like such extremely high temperatures they're called hyperthermophiles ("hyper" means "excessively"). Others, called psychrophiles, prefer intensely cold places, like Antarctica. Halophiles inhabit extremely salty places, like the Dead Sea. Acidophiles like places with a low pH, which means the environment is acidic. Alkaliphiles prefer the opposite. They live where the pH is high.

How can archaea live in so many different environments? For one thing, some can "eat"

A Revolution in Biology

In 1977, Carl Woese published an article about archaea. He wrote that almost ten years of research had demonstrated they were so different from bacteria and eukaryotes that they constituted a third domain. Many scientists said that couldn't be true. The idea that the tree of life had two domains—Bacteria and Eukarya—was well established and must be right. However, it was wrong, and Woese was right. Woese's discovery forced scientists to create a new tree of life and rethink how life developed on Earth and how organisms are related to each other. It started a revolution that hasn't ended.

inorganic materials such as iron, sulfur, carbon dioxide, hydrogen, ammonia, uranium, and other substances that are toxic to humans. Think about that for a minute. Archaea can use iron to make nutrients. No person could manage that feat!

Groups of Archaea

Biologists are still debating the number of major Archaea groups. At least two exist: Crenarchaeota and Euryarchaeota.

Crenarchaeota may be the most common. They include the archaea living in the hottest places. One type prefers temperatures high enough to sterilize surgical instruments! Others, called thermoacidophiles, like hot, acid environments. Still others live in cool ocean waters. Many soil microbes that convert ammonia into nitrites belong to Crenarchaeota.

Euryarchaeota has three main groups. The methanogens produce methane gas. They live in anaerobic environments such as swamps, animal digestive systems, and sewage. Halophiles love salty habitats like the Dead Sea and salt ponds at the south end of San Francisco Bay. Euryarchaeota's thermoacidophiles don't like as much heat as Crenarchaeota's. They live in places like Yellowstone National Park's sulfur springs.

Biologists debate how to classify Korarchaeota and Nanoarchaeota. Some believe Korarchaeota form a subbranch of Crenarchaeota. However, others think its members are very ancient ancestors of Crenarchaeota, Euryarchaeota, and Eukarya. That's because genome sequencing revealed that one type possesses genes long believed distinctive to these other groups.

Then there are the Nanoarchaeota. They're called "nano" because they're so small. They're the tiniest microbes yet discovered—about four hundred nanometers in diameter. How small is that? A nanometer is much smaller than a micrometer. The head of a pin has a diameter

Many hot springs in Yellowstone National Park, such as the one shown here, display dazzling colors. The colors result from minerals deposited by the extremophiles that inhabit the hot springs.

of about one million nanometers! Nanoarchaeota seem to be parasites. They lack genes for digestion.

Structure of Archaea

In many ways, archaea resemble bacteria. That's why they were first
considered weird bacteria.

A membrane and cell wall surround most archaea. A capsule
encloses everything. A flagellum and pili may be attached to the
outside. The interior holds cytoplasm with ribosomes, a nucleoid,
plasmids, and storage bodies (called granules rather than inclusions,
as the storage bodies in bacteria are called).

So what makes archaea different from bacteria? Archaea have
some distinctive shapes. Some are spheres, rods, or spirals, like bacteria. However, others are extremely thin filaments. Some rod-shaped
archaea are almost perfect rectangles. One species is flat and
square. Others are triangular. Some have no cell wall to hold a
shape, so they're irregular, much like an ameba.

Archaea also differ from bacteria in important chemical ways.
For example, their cell walls lack the peptidoglycan in bacteria
cell walls. Archaean membranes and flagella also have different
chemicals. Their storage bodies hold different material. Archaean
ribosomes act more like those of humans than those of bacteria! In
addition, archaea differ from bacteria genetically.

Archaean Genetics

In 1996, *Methanococcus jannaschii* became the first archaean to
have its genome sequenced. As more archaea were sequenced,
scientists learned that archaea possess many genes not found in
bacteria or eukaryotes. They also discovered that archaean genomes
contain inactive DNA segments called introns. Such segments exist in

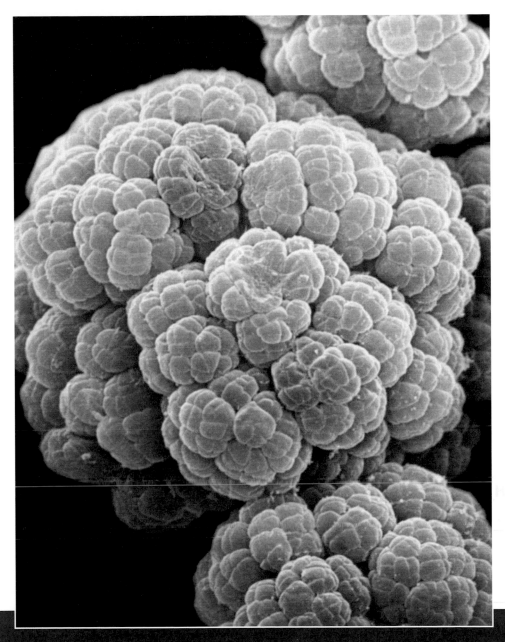

It's easy to see why archaea were originally considered a type of bacteria. Structurally, they are similar. It takes chemical analysis and genome sequencing to make the differences clear.

eukaryotes but not in bacteria. In addition, scientists found that the process by which archaea utilize DNA and RNA to produce proteins resembles that in eukaryotes more than that in bacteria.

Reproduction in archaea, like that in bacteria, occurs through binary fission, budding, or fragmentation. Such asexual reproduction limits genetic variation in a species. However, archaea can also exchange plasmids in a process similar to conjugation in bacteria. In addition, as scientists learned more about microbial genetics, they found something strange. They discovered that genes were actually transferred from one organism to another! This didn't just occur between organisms within one domain but between organisms in different domains as well. Imagine that. Genes being transferred not just from one organism to a similar one, but from one organism to a very different one. This phenomenon is called horizontal, or lateral, gene transfer. It still occurs and has huge implications for understanding the beginning and development of life on Earth.

CHAPTER six

Plentiful Protista: Protozoans, Algae, and More

Protists, remember, are eukaryotes. They encompass almost all unicellular organisms that aren't prokaryotes (such as yeasts). As chapter 2 noted, modern science has shown they're not closely related.

Protists include a stunning variety of organisms, some of which were formerly considered plants, animals, or fungi. Others hadn't been discovered before the term "protist" was invented. Most are unicellular. Even multicellular protists have only one kind of tissue, unlike other eukaryotes. Still, the organisms aren't closely related. The terms "protist" and "Protista" continue to be used simply because it's easier than saying "eukaryotes that aren't animals, plants, or fungi."

Protist Lifestyle

Like other microbes, protists are among Earth's oldest life-forms. Algae helped increase the oxygen in Earth's atmosphere, making the development of modern life-forms possible.

Science writer Leslie Mullen reports that about two hundred thousand protist species have been identified, and millions may exist. Protists may be free living, symbiotic, or parasitic. Free-living forms fill oceans, freshwater bodies, swimming pools, and sewage treatment plants. They inhabit soil, forest floors, deserts, and trees. Symbiotic protists live in association with animals, plants, fungi, and even other protists. Hundreds of thousands may dwell in a single termite's gut! Parasites harm animals and plants.

Many protists carry on photosynthesis, but others get their energy from food. Most protists are aerobic. However, parasites as well as some other species live where they must be able to function anaerobically.

A mother tries to comfort her five-year-old son, who is ill with malaria. Most of those who die of malaria in Africa are infants and children.

The Bad and the Good

People classify protists as "bad" when they endanger human life. The microbes, of course, are simply trying to stay alive.

A parasitic protist causes the disease malaria. Although malaria is treatable today, it wasn't always. Biologist John Kimball estimates it has killed more people than any other infectious disease. Treatment still isn't available everywhere, and perhaps a million people in Africa die annually.

Other parasitic protists cause African sleeping sickness in humans and various animal diseases. Some funguslike protists attack plants. A famous example comes from Ireland in the 1840s, when a protist

Coral reefs provide homes for a rich array of organisms. The coral that build reefs depend on algae living in them for essential nutrients. Without the algae, they die.

destroyed the potato crop, causing a famine. Another protist killed so many grapes in France that it nearly ruined the French wine industry.

Yet many protists are beneficial. They help maintain the atmospheric balance of oxygen and carbon dioxide. They're important marine decomposers and nutrient recyclers. Symbiotic protists inside coral animals make possible the spectacular coral reefs, where a rich variety of life-forms live. Some marine protists leave behind shells that help create limestone, which people use in construction.

Protist Groups

There are a number of distinct protist groups, only distantly related to each other. Let's look at several to get some sense of their variety and complexity.

Protozoans

"Protozoa" means "first animals," and scientists first thought of these microbes as simple animals from which later animals evolved. Some possess animal-like features such as a mouth or an eyespot that senses light and dark. However, others possess the pigment chlorophyll and carry out photosynthesis, like plants. Today, scientists no longer consider protozoans to belong to a single group and don't use the term in the scientific classification system. However, the term is still widely used for general audiences.

Tens of thousands of species exist. They live in moist places. Millions inhabit bodies of water, where they recycle nutrients and clean the water by eating bacteria. In turn, they're food for other small organisms.

Protozoans may be grouped based on how they move. Flagellates use flagella to move. Some have chloroplasts and conduct photosynthesis. Others eat other organisms. Some are parasites, such as the flagellate that causes African sleeping sickness. Sarcodines move by means of pseudopods, or false feet, which they form by creating

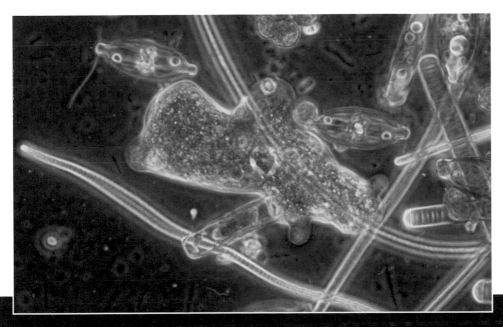

Two groups of protists appear in this image: sarcodines, which are protozoans, and diatoms, which are algae with hard, glasslike shells.

fingerlike projections. Amebas and foraminifera (the protists whose shells help form limestone) belong to this group. Apicomplexans move by gliding. Parasites, including the malaria parasite, comprise this group. The most complex protozoans are the ciliates. Fine hairlike cilia cover them, helping them move and capture food. Paramecia, science-class favorites, are ciliates.

Algae

Algae are simple organisms inhabiting salt water, freshwater, and moist soil. While some are quite large—kelp can reach about 200 feet (60 meters)—the focus here is on microscopic algae. Unlike "protozoa," "algae" is a useful descriptive term still accepted; however, it's important to realize that the organisms called "algae" aren't closely related.

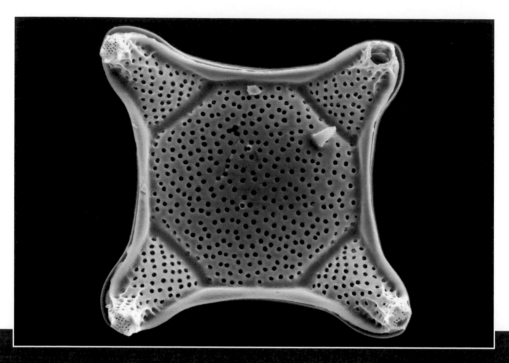

The word "algae" often makes people picture grasslike forms. Microscopic algae come in a wide range of forms. The shapes of diatoms, such as the ones shown here, are especially varied and exquisite.

Algae have chloroplasts and carry out photosynthesis. They provide much of the world's oxygen and form the bottom of the food chain for nearly all marine and freshwater life.

Algae may be red, green, or brown, depending on the pigment in their chloroplasts. Generally, microscopic algae are green. Most live in freshwater. They come in many shapes. Some have two or more flagella. Others have none. One tiny symbiotic type has become a popular health food because of its rich protein and chlorophyll content.

Other microscopic algae include freshwater golden algae. Most are photosynthetic. However, if there's insufficient light, they may feed on other microbes! Diatoms get a golden-brown color from their green and yellow-orange pigments. They differ from other algae in having a hard, glasslike frustule (skeleton) made of silica. Frustules come in a variety of beautiful, intricate shapes.

Funguslike Protists and Some Others

The funguslike protists encompass water molds and slime molds. Water molds are, in fact, very distant relatives of fungi. Slime molds, however, are unrelated to fungi, although they're distant relatives of water molds.

Water molds include the microbe that caused the Irish potato famine and those that attack grapes. Some are fish and amphibian parasites. Another water mold is killing California oak trees.

Other funguslike protists are slime molds. Cellular slime molds spend most of their lives as unicellular organisms. At certain times, however, thousands gather in a swarm. Plasmodial slime molds also

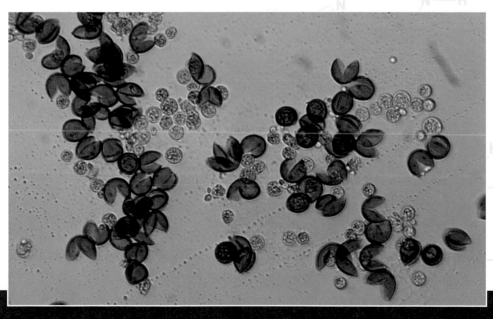

These slime-mold-forming spores are releasing cells to begin a new generation. Each cell has only half the normal number of genes and will combine with another cell to form a complete organism.

have a life-cycle stage when thousands come together. Unlike their cellular cousins, however, the individual cells don't remain separate. Instead, they unite in a single giant cell with thousands of nuclei.

Other protists lack mitochondria, the power plant of eukaryotic cells, although they appear to be descendants of earlier protists that did possess mitochondria. Parasitic *Giardia*, for example, infect people's intestines and can cause diarrhea. Parabasalians living inside animals may cause disease, coexist with the host symbiotically, or have no effect on the host. Pelobiontids use symbiotic bacteria to compensate for their missing mitochondria.

Genetics

As this chapter has indicated, scientists still have much to learn about protists, and many disagreements must be resolved. Genomic analysis has already revealed important information. Studies of protists without mitochondria suggest they may form one of the eukaryotic tree's earliest branches. The gene sequences of ciliates, apicomplexans, and dinoflagellates imply they share a common ancestor.

Genetic analysis also revealed an important difference between water molds and fungi. The gene sequences of water molds differ significantly from those of fungi. They resemble much more closely the sequences of diatoms and golden and brown algae. Furthermore, water molds, diatoms, and brown algae have genes very similar to those in both green and red algae.

Finally, there's a group of flagellates called choanoflagellates because of the collar ("choano") around their flagella. Although they're unicellular, they have genes for several proteins crucial to interactions between cells in complex multicellular animals. These microbes are in fact the closest protist relatives to people.

CHAPTER seven

Viruses: Invisible Invaders

Everyone's had a viral disease like a cold or the flu. Yet how much do most people know about viruses?

Viruses are the tiniest microbes, invisible even with the best compound microscope. The largest is about 1/10 the size of the average bacterium. The smallest is about 0.01 micrometer. It would take about two and a half *million* to equal one inch!

Viruses are everywhere and have existed for millions of years. They're built to live as parasites in plants, animals (including people), and bacteria. They cause deadly diseases like smallpox, AIDS, and some cancers. Even "ordinary" diseases like the flu can be fatal. Yet viruses have also played a critical role in the development of life on Earth.

What makes viruses so dangerous? Viruses' structure is part of the reason.

Structure of Viruses

Unlike other organisms, viruses aren't composed of cells. A virus is just genetic material—DNA or, sometimes, RNA—enclosed in a

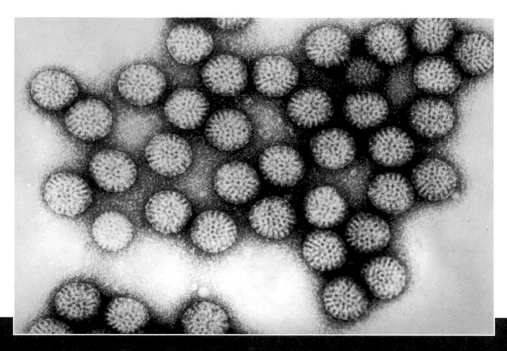

Each of these viruses has a double capsid. The radiating capsomeres that make up the capsids give the viruses their distinctive appearance.

protein coat. There's nothing else—no cytoplasm, plasmids, ribosomes, inclusions, granules, or organelles.

Proteins called capsomeres comprise the coat, or capsid, which provides the virus's shape. Some viruses are polyhedral, or multi-sided. Some are roughly oval. Others look like long, skinny sticks or bits of string. Some even resemble a lunar landing vehicle!

The capsid protects the vital inner genetic material. Sometimes an additional protective envelope of proteins, fats, and carbohydrates surrounds the capsid. Some envelopes have spikes that help the virus attach to host cells.

The virus's structure presents a question: Are viruses alive? They can't reproduce—an activity associated with living organisms. Yet once inside a host cell, a virus's nucleic acid takes over the cell's machinery and can reproduce rapidly. So is it alive or not? Scientists still don't agree.

How Viruses Work

Most viruses require specific host cells. A virus recognizes its host through receptors on the host's exterior. Receptors help the virus bind to the host. The virus injects its nucleic acid into the host, takes command, and reproduces.

Viruses reproduce by two methods—the lytic cycle and the lysogenic cycle. In the lytic cycle, the host's DNA is destroyed, the viral DNA takes over, and the cell lyses (bursts), releasing a new generation of viruses. In the lysogenic cycle, the viral DNA or RNA becomes part of the host DNA, and the host cell may divide many times, carrying the viral nucleic acid, without any cell dying.

The lytic cycle causes disease in the host. The lysogenic cycle doesn't. Sometimes, however, a virus switches from the lysogenic to the lytic cycle.

Certain RNA viruses—called retroviruses—contain an enzyme called reverse transcriptase.

Viroids and Virusoids

Viroids and virusoids are the smallest, simplest viruses. They're just genetic material without a capsid. Viroids cause diseases in plant cells, but their lack of a capsid makes it difficult for them to spread to another plant or even another cell. Virusoids must insert themselves into a "helper" virus to reproduce, much like viruses require host cells to reproduce.

It allows virus RNA to make a DNA copy of itself inside the host. This becomes a permanent part of the host's genome.

Because most viruses reproduce rapidly, there's increased chance for mutations. That's a good survival mechanism for viruses because it can produce viruses resistant to traditional treatments. However, it's bad news for hosts. It means they're constantly besieged by new viruses.

Mutations can also enable viruses to jump from one species to another. The 2009 H1N1 (swine flu virus) is one example.

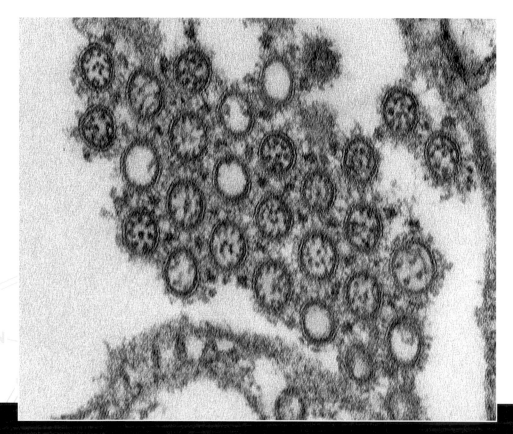

The 2009 H1N1 virus was invisible to the average person, but it certainly had an enormous impact. Here's the organism that caused the commotion. Each individual oval is a virus.

Scientists examined its genes after it first appeared in humans. Early tests showed it possessed genes similar to those normally seen in flu viruses of North American pigs. However, further study revealed two genes from flu viruses normally found in European and Asian pigs, bird genes, and human genes. This virus had jumped around a lot!

Viral Diseases

Quick! Name some viral diseases. It won't be difficult. The list is long. As mentioned at the beginning of the chapter, the "common cold" is one—or, more accurately, several. Almost one hundred types of rhinovirus (from the Greek word for nose, *rhis*) exist! Researchers finally completed sequencing the DNA of all these in 2009.

Viruses cause chicken pox, measles, and mumps, too. As already mentioned, they also cause influenza, or flu. Up to sixty million people in the United States get the flu annually. Most recover. However, flu can lead to more serious illnesses and even result in death. Very young children, the elderly, and people with suppressed immune systems are most at risk. That's why people are encouraged to get yearly flu shots.

Most Americans today probably aren't familiar with poliomyelitis— polio for short. This terrible viral disease once paralyzed or killed tens of thousands of people. Today, vaccines can prevent polio.

Dreadful viral diseases called hemorrhagic fevers are most common in Africa. Patients experience flulike symptoms, then develop internal and external bleeding (hemorrhaging). Up to 90 percent of patients die. The best-known hemorrhagic fever is Ebola.

Herpes viruses receive a lot of attention today. People often think there are two kinds. Actually, at least twenty-five kinds exist and at least eight infect humans. Herpes viruses cause cold sores and the disease called infectious mononucleosis. They can also cause sores

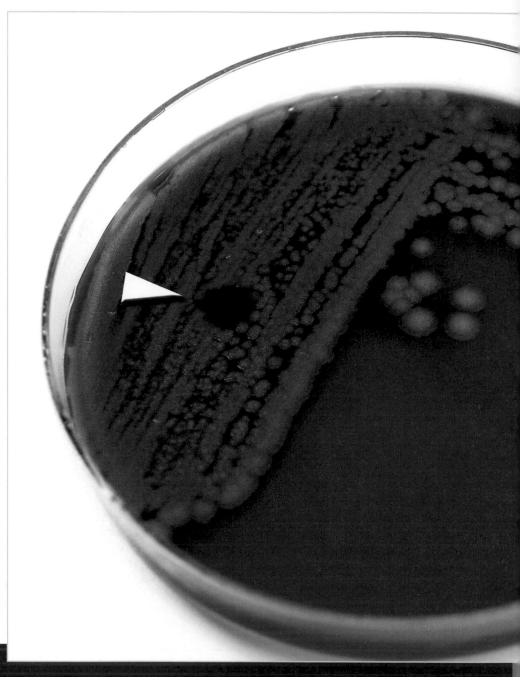

This dish contains Bacillus anthracis *grown in a laboratory. The arrow points to a dark spot where the bacteria were destroyed by bacteriophages added to the dish.*

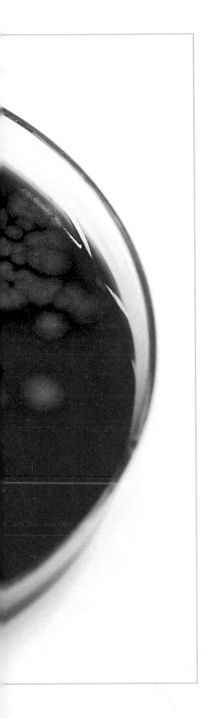

on the chest, face, eyes, and sexual organs. They can even cause a serious brain infection that may be fatal.

HIV, or human immunodeficiency virus, also receives a lot of attention. It's the retrovirus that causes AIDS (acquired immunodeficiency syndrome). People with AIDS have severely weakened immune systems. They become ill easily, have difficulty fighting diseases, and are more likely to get rare, often fatal, diseases. Scientists finally decoded HIV's genome in 2009.

Viruses cause hundreds of animal diseases. One example is canine distemper, which causes serious illness and sometimes death in puppies. A virus causes foot-and-mouth (hoof-and-mouth) disease in cattle, sheep, and pigs. Infected animals develop painful blisters in and around their mouth and above their hooves. Adults rarely die, but young animals may. Viruses are also responsible for cowpox, rabies, and some animal cancers.

Viruses infect all kinds of plants, too. Remember how viruses were discovered? Beijerinck and Ivanovski were studying a tobacco plant disease. Viruses also attack flowers and all sorts of fruits and vegetables. The list is almost endless.

Viruses even infect bacteria. These are called bacteriophages, or phages for short. ("Phage" comes from a Greek word meaning "one who eats.") Phages often kill their bacterial hosts, although some coexist in a lysogenic cycle. Like all microbes, phages are everywhere. How many are there? According to the American Society for Microbiology, the weight of all the phages on Earth is more than one thousand times the total weight of the world's elephant population!

Benefits from Viruses

Believe it or not, viruses have also provided benefits. They've actually contributed to the development of life on Earth. Remember the mixture of genes in the H1N1 virus? It demonstrates how viruses redistribute

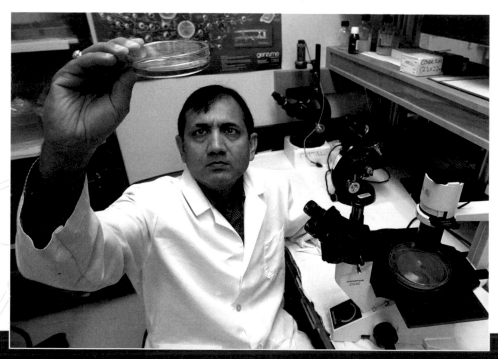

Because mutations constantly produce new viruses, scientists are continually searching for vaccines to protect against them. This researcher at Purdue University in Indiana is working on a vaccine for avian flu.

genes among organisms. Because genes are the basic units of heredity, such activity shapes how organisms change and evolve.

Scientists today find viruses useful for several purposes.
Virologists—the scientists who study viruses—are working on ways
to use viruses instead of insecticides to protect crops. Insecticides
can harm plants and other animals. Viruses specific to particular
insect pests could be used to kill them without harming other organisms. Scientists also use viruses to develop vaccines and other drugs.
Finally, viruses are extremely useful in genetic research because of
their simple structure. Biologists have used bacteriophages to study
genes and DNA. Remember the discussion about conservation of
genes across species at the beginning of the book? That means the
research on bacteriophages gives scientists genetic knowledge that
can be applied to all organisms.

Just as research on phage genetics provides insight into all
organisms, so does research on the genetics of all microbes.
Because microbes live everywhere—even in places where scientists
long thought life was impossible—they help scientists develop
greater understanding of life in general. This knowledge can help
with the search for life beyond Earth. It may lead to new ideas for
medical treatments, fuels, or robotics. It may lead science in direc-
tions not even imagined yet. Microbes may be tiny, but their
importance is huge.

Glossary

antibiotics Substances produced by some microbes and fungi that kill other microbes or slow their growth. They are especially useful in treating infections caused by bacteria but not viruses.

chromosome A structure, containing genes, that is passed from parent to offspring.

decomposers Organisms that break down dead organisms and recycle nutrients.

digestion The process of breaking down food into simpler chemical compounds that can be absorbed and used by an organism.

domain The highest rank of organisms, higher than a kingdom.

electrons Tiny, negatively charged particles that orbit the positively charged nucleus of an atom.

enzymes Complex proteins that regulate the rates of biochemical reactions in an organism.

epidemics Outbreaks of diseases that affect a large number of people in an area at the same time.

eukaryote Any organism with one or more cells that have visible nuclei and organelles.

filaments Very long, thin, cylindrical cells.

genome All the genetic information in an organism.

heredity Transmission of information from one generation to the next through genes.

immune Having a high degree of resistance to a disease.

membrane A thin, flexible layer that allows some things, but not others, to pass through.

methane A colorless, odorless, flammable gas resulting from the decomposition of organic matter; it is also produced by some archaea.

micrometers (microns) Units of measure equal to one-millionth of a meter. A micrometer equals 0.000039 inch.

mutation A random change in a gene or chromosome that results in a new trait that can be inherited.

nutrients Matter organisms need to live and grow.

parasites Organisms that live in association with other organisms, obtaining advantages from the other organisms while usually harming them.

pH Measure of how acidic or basic a solution is. Values below 7 are acidic; values above 7 are basic.

photosynthesis The process by which plants and some microbes produce food using air, sunlight, and water.

prokaryote An organism whose DNA is not contained within a nucleus; for example, a bacterium.

pus Thick, yellowish white fluid formed by the body in reaction to infection.

receptors Protein molecules that recognize and bind specific small molecules such as hormones.

silica A chemical compound composed of silicon and oxygen; it is the principal component of glass.

sterilize To free from living microbes, typically by heating.

taxon A group to which organisms are assigned according to the principles of taxonomy, including species, genus, family, order, class, and phylum.

For More Information

American Society for Microbiology (ASM)
1752 N Street NW
Washington, DC 20036-2904
(202) 737-3600
Web site: http://www.asm.org
The society's mission is to advance microbiology as a way to understand
    life processes, and to apply and communicate this knowledge world-
    wide for the improvement of health and for environmental and
    economic well-being.

American Society of Parasitologists (ASP)
c/o John Janovy Jr., Secretary-Treasurer
Varner Professor of Biological Sciences
School of Biological Sciences
University of Nebraska–Lincoln
Lincoln, NE 68588-0118
(402) 472-2754
Web site: http://asp.unl.edu
The ASP is actively involved in public policy issues important to biology
    and the environment. Issues include conservation of biological diver-
    sity, the use of animals in laboratory research, and clinical laboratory
    standards.

American Society for Virology (ASV)
c/o Dr. Dorothea L. Sawicki
Secretary-Treasurer, ASV
Department of Medical Microbiology and Immunology
Health Science Campus
University of Toledo College of Medicine

3000 Arlington Avenue, Mail Stop 1021
Toledo, OH 43614-2598
(419) 383-5173
Web site: http://www.asv.org/contact.html
The ASV provides a forum for investigators of human, animal, insect, plant, fungal, and bacterial viruses. The society's aim is to promote the exchange of information and stimulate discussion and collaboration among scientists active in all aspects of virology.

Association of Medical Microbiology and Infectious Disease
Canada (AMMI)
298 Elgin Street, Suite 101
Ottawa, ON K2P 1M3
Canada
(613) 260-3233
Web site: http://www.ammi.ca
The association's mission is to contribute to the health of people at risk of, or affected by, infectious diseases; support research and education in infectious diseases and medical microbiology; and develop guidelines and policies for the prevention, diagnosis, and management of infectious diseases.

Canadian Association for Clinical Microbiology and Infectious
Diseases (CACMID)
c/o Dr. Karam Ramotar, President
Medical Microbiologist
The Ottawa Hospital, General Campus
501 Smyth Road
Ottawa, ON K1H 8L6
Canada
(613) 737-8899 x74748
Web site: http://www.cacmid.ca

The CACMID works to promote cooperation among professionals in clinical microbiology and infectious disease; to promote education, research, and interchange of ideas within the professional body; and to develop and promote standards and guidelines in clinical microbiology.

Canadian Society of Microbiologists
CSM-SCM Secretariat
c/o Rofail Conference and Management Services
17 Dossetter Way
Ottawa, ON K1G 4S3
Canada
(613) 482-2654
Web site: http://www.csm-scm.org
Founded in 1952, the Canadian Society of Microbiologists seeks to advance microbiology in all its aspects and to facilitate the interchange of ideas between microbiologists.

Centers for Disease Control and Prevention
Office of Public Health Genomics
1600 Clifton Road
Atlanta, GA 30333
(800) 232-4636
Web site: http://www.cdc.gov
The Office of Public Health Genomics was founded in 1997 to help incorporate genomics into public health research, policy, and programs.

Genetics Society of America (GSA)
9650 Rockville Pike
Bethesda, MD 20814-3998
(301) 634-7300
(866) HUMGENE (486-4363)

Web site: http://www.genetics-gsa.org
The GSA works to improve communication between geneticists, promote
  research, foster the training of the next generation of geneticists, and
  educate the public and government about advances in genetics and
  their consequences to individuals and society.

Microscopy Society of America (MSA)
12100 Sunset Hills Road, Suite 130
Reston, VA 20190
(800) 538-3672 or (703) 234-4115
Web site: http://www.microscopy.org
Founded in 1942, the MSA is dedicated to the promotion and advance-
  ment of techniques and applications of microscopy and microanalysis
  in all relevant scientific disciplines.

Web Sites

Due to the changing nature of Internet links, Rosen Publishing has developed
an online list of Web sites related to the subject of this book. This site is
updated regularly. Please use this link to access the list:

http://www.rosenlinks.com/gen/bact

For Further Reading

Buckman, Robert. *Human Wildlife: The Life That Lives on Us*. Baltimore, MD: Johns Hopkins University Press, 2003.

Burdass, Dariel Anne. *The Good, the Bad, & the Ugly: Microbes*. Reading, England: Society for General Microbiology, 2009.

Ingraham, John L. *March of the Microbes: Sighting the Unseen*. Cambridge, MA: Belknap Press, 2010.

Jones, Phillip. *The Genetic Code* (Science Foundations). New York, NY: Chelsea House, 2010.

Sheehan, Kathy B., David J. Patterson, Brett Leigh Dicks, and Joan M. Henson. *Seen and Unseen: Discovering the Microbes of Yellowstone*. Guilford, CT: Falcon, 2005.

White, Mary E. *Earth Alive! From Microbes to a Living Planet*. Dural Delivery Centre, Australia: Rosenberg Publishing, 2003.

Zimmer, Carl. *Microcosm: E. coli and the New Science of Life*. New York, NY: Vintage Books, 2009.

Bibliography

American Society of Microbiology. "Division M: Bacteriophage." Retrieved August 22, 2009 (http://www.asm.org/division/m/M.html).

Ben-Barak, Idan. *The Invisible Kingdom: From the Tips of Our Fingers to the Tops of Our Trash, Inside the Curious World of Microbes.* New York, NY: Basic Books, 2009.

Bennett, Jim, Michael Cooper, Michael Hunter, and Lisa Jardine. *London's Leonardo: The Life and Work of Robert Hooke.* New York, NY: Oxford University Press, 2003.

Carucci, Daniel J., Malcolm J. Gardner, Herve Tettelin, et al. "The Malaria Genome Sequencing Project." *Expert Reviews in Molecular Medicine,* Vol. 1, No. 3, May 1998, pp. 1–9.

Crawford, Dorothy H. *Deadly Companions: How Microbes Shaped Our History.* New York, NY: Oxford University Press, 2007.

Crawford, Dorothy H. *The Invisible Enemy: A Natural History of Viruses.* New York, NY: Oxford University Press, 2000.

Farrell, Jeanette. *Invisible Allies: Microbes That Shape Our Lives.* New York, NY: Farrar, Straus and Giroux, 2005.

Friend, Tim. *The Third Domain: The Untold Story of Archaea and the Future of Biotechnology.* Washington, DC: Joseph Henry Press, 2007.

Kimball, John W. "Kimball's Biology Pages." Retrieved August 22, 2009 (http://users.rcn.com/jkimball.ma.ultranet/BiologyPages).

Lechevalier, Hubert. "Dmitri Iosifovich Ivanovski (1864–1920)." *Bacteriological Reviews,* Vol. 36, No. 2, June 1972, pp. 135–145.

Levy, Janey. *Alopecia Areata* (Genetic Diseases and Disorders). New York, NY: Rosen Publishing Group, 2007.

Lowy, Frank. "Bacterial Classification, Structure and Function." Columbia University. Lecture notes. Retrieved August 22, 2009 (http://www.columbia.edu/itc/hs/medical/pathophys/id/2009/introNotes.pdf).

Microscope.com. "Compound Microscope History." The Microscope Store, LLC. Retrieved August 30, 2009 (http://www.microscope.com/compound-microscope-history-t-4.html).

Mullen, Leslie. "The Life That Spawned a Quarter-Million Descendant Species." *Astrobiology Magazine*, 2002. Retrieved October 2, 2009 (http://www.astrobio.net/exclusive/298/the-life-that-spawned-a-quarter-million-descendant-species).

The Paper Project. "History of the Microscope." Retrieved August 30, 2009 (http://paperproject.org/microscopehistory/index.html).

Waggoner, Ben. "Antony van Leeuwenhoek (1632–1723)." University of California Museum of Paleontology, 1996. Retrieved July 29, 2009 (http://www.ucmp.berkeley.edu/history/leeuwenhoek.html).

Waggoner, Ben. "Archaea: Morphology." University of California Museum of Paleontology, 1994. Retrieved September 2, 2009 (http://www.usmp.berkeley.edu/archaea/archaeamm.html).

Waggoner, Ben. "Robert Hooke (1635–1703)." University of California Museum of Paleontology, 2001. Retrieved August 28, 2009 (http://www.ucmp.berkeley.edu/history/hooke.html).

Woese, Carl. "Interpreting the Universal Phylogenetic Tree." *Proceedings of the National Academy of Sciences*, Vol. 97, No. 15, July 18, 2000, pp. 8,392–8,396.

Index

About the Author

Janey Levy is a writer and editor who lives in Colden, New York. She has written more than one hundred books for readers ranging in age from kindergarten to young adult. Among the subjects her books have covered are numerous science topics, including chemistry, ecosystems, and genetic diseases.

Photo Credits:

Cover (top) Dr. Stanley Flegler/Visuals Unlimited/Getty Images; cover (bottom), back cover, and interior © www.istockphoto.com/Gregory Spencer; pp. 5, 20 Dr. Terence Beveridge/Visuals Unlimited/Getty Images; p. 8 U.S. Department of Energy Genome Programs (http://genomics.energy.gov); p. 9 Photo Researchers, Inc.; p. 12 Dr. Stan Erlandsen/CDC; p. 13 SPL/Photo Researchers, Inc.; p. 17 Ralph Slepecky/Visuals Unlimited, Inc.; p. 18 Getty Images; p. 21 Image courtesy of NOAA Ocean Explorer: Submarine Ring of Fire 2006. Adapted from C. R. Woese, O. Kandler, and M. L. Wheelis, Towards a natural system of organisms. June 1990; p. 23 AFP/Getty Images; p. 25 Three Lions/Hulton Archive/Getty Images; p. 27 Courtesy of the National Library of Medicine; p. 29 Hulton Archive/Getty Images; p. 31 Ethan Miller/Getty Images; p. 32 © AP Images; pp. 35, 36, 47, 53 Shutterstock.com; p. 40 Janice Haney Carr/CDC; p. 44 Eye of Science/Photo Researchers, Inc.; p. 49 Ralph Robinson/Visuals Unlimited/Getty Images; p. 52 Cris Bouroncle/AFP/Getty Images; p. 55 M. I. Walker/Photo Researchers, Inc; p. 56 G. Wanner/ScienceFoto/Getty Images; p. 57 Paul Zahl/National Geographic/Getty Images; p. 60 Bryon Skinner/CDC; p. 62 Cynthia Goldsmith/CDC; pp. 64–65 CDC; p. 66 Jeff Haynes/AFP/Getty Images.

Designer: Nicole Russo; Editor: Kathy Kuhtz Campbell;
Photo Researcher: Cindy Reiman